I0163086

7 Days of

Fasting and Prayer

The Point of Prayer is the
Prayer Point!

SARAH MORGAN

Copyright © 2016 SARAH MORGAN

ISBN: 978-0-9859690-6-6

MORGAN PUBLISHING
The Pen of a Ready Writer

7 Days of Fasting and Prayer: The Point of Prayer is the Prayer Point!

Published by Morgan Publishing

P.O. Box 470047

Los Angeles, CA 90047

1 (800)-320-5622 ext. 1

JOIN THE MOVEMENT! CONNECT WITH US ON:

www.womenofvisionla.org

www.periscope.com/womenofvisionla

www.facebook.com/officialwomenofvisionla

www.twitter.com/womenofvisionla

ISBN 978-0-9859690-6-6

Cover Design by Dee Shervell

Editing and typesetting by Fresh Reign Publishing | www.freshreign.com

Dedication

This is dedicated to all praying warriors, intercessors, travailing women and wayfaring men in Gods Army. Your seasons of fasting and prayer have changed the course of your generation more than you will ever know. I pray that generations yet unborn will encounter GOD because of your sacrifice.

"God is not unjust, He will not forget your work and labor of love, which ye have shewed toward His name, in that ye have ministered to the saints, and do minister" (Hebrews 6:1).

Yours truly,

Sarah Morgan

Table of Contents

Preface

These Prayer Point books came out of a season of consecration through fasting and prayer, which is annually observed by *Prayer Academy* students across the country to end the year strong.

At the end of last year in October, I was led by the Holy Spirit to extend this invitation to the nation, via the medium of *Periscope* where intercessors and prayer warriors joined me to pray daily on our beloved broadcast *Prayer Altar Scope* where we gather at the *Altar to be Altered*. This army of Praying Warriors and Intercessors grew exponentially and continues to grow by the Grace of God.

Since that first cooperate fast, the *Prayer Altar Scope* family has observed several fasts together praying for families, relationships, marriages, churches, communities, cities, regions, our nation and the world standing on 2 Chronicles 7:14-15: *"If My people, who are called by My name, shall humble themselves, pray, seek, crave, and require of necessity My face and turn from their wicked ways, then will I hear from heaven, forgive their sin, and heal their land. Now My eyes will be open and My ears attentive to prayer offered in this place."* What place was God speaking about? *The place of Prayer is the Place of Power.*

In order for everyone to pray the same thing from their respective regions, cities and states, through the medium of technology and social media e.g. our Facebook:

@officialwomenofvisionla, our website: www.womenofvisionla.org, and our Twitter: @womenofvisionla; we loaded the Prayer Points daily with the help of Prophetess Karla Allen, AKA, Coach K~ [Shout out to Coach K~].

Consequently, as we gathered daily at the prayer altar, the seekers requested that we put the prayer points in print for future seasons of prayer and fasting, individually and corporately. Hence, our newest additions to our prayer arsenal, *The Point of Prayer is The Prayer Point* series:

1. 7 Days of Fasting and Prayer
2. 21 Days of Fasting and Prayer
3. 30 Days of Fasting and Prayer

Remember, "Anything that is not birthed out of prayer is Illegal."

Yours Truly,

Sarah Morgan

Introduction

"Fight the good fight of faith . . ." (1 Timothy 6:12).

Throughout history, God has called on His people to humble themselves through fasting and prayer. Fasting is a spiritual weapon God uses to advance His kingdom, change the destiny of nations, spark a revival, and bring victory in people's lives. There is something powerful that happens when we voluntarily humble ourselves, seek God's will and agree with Him for His purposes to be fulfilled.

As a spiritual family of Praying Warriors and Watchmen on the Wall, we purpose to begin and end each year with a season of prayer and fasting.

It is our way of humbling ourselves before God and consecrating to Him the approaching New Year and thanking Him for crowning the year with goodness. It is also the time when we corporately come into agreement and believe together for breakthroughs in our personal lives, families, finances, and churches.

Over the years, as a result of this time of prayer, I have seen people receive healing, salvation, promotion, direction, family restoration, miraculous provision, and tremendous growth in their fellowships and churches. One of the highlights is always seeing and hearing testimonies of how God answers over and beyond what His people ask.

As you begin your fast, believe in your heart, by faith, that this year is your year of miracles and answered prayers.

"Declare a holy fast; call a sacred assembly. Summon the elders and all who live in the land to the house of the LORD your God, and cry out to the LORD" (Joel 1:14).

"Consecrate yourselves, for tomorrow the LORD will do amazing things among you" (Joshua 3:5).

Believe God for victories and breakthroughs in every area of your life as you begin and end the year strong in Jesus name.

When a man is willing to set aside the legitimate appetites of the body to concentrate on the work of praying, he is demonstrating that he means business, he is seeking with all his heart and will not let God go unless He answers.

Practical Prayer and Fasting Guide

1. Jesus fasted.

"Then Jesus was led by the Spirit into the desert to be tempted by the devil. After fasting forty days and forty nights, he was hungry" (Matthew 4:1-2).

"Jesus returned to Galilee in the power of the Spirit, and news about him spread through the whole countryside" (Luke 4:14).

    a.   Before He began His ministry, Jesus fasted forty days and ate nothing. He knew He was going to need spiritual strength and stamina to fulfill His purposes. Fasting makes us physically weak, but spiritually strong and prepares us to do God's work.

8

2. Fasting is an act of humility and consecration.

". . . I put on sackcloth and humbled myself with fasting. . ."
(Psalm 35:13).

> a. Humility results in the grace of God. When
> we humble ourselves in prayer, we have
> instant access to the heart of God. As we
> deny ourselves as an act of consecration, we
> are better able to exercise self-control in the
> areas of our desires and emotions.

**3. Fasting helps us become sensitive to the Holy
Spirit.**

*"While they were worshiping the Lord and fasting, the Holy
Spirit said, "Set apart for me Barnabas and Saul for the
work to which I have called them" (Acts 13:2).*

> *a.* When we deny ourselves of our natural
> cravings, our spiritual antennas become
> sharper. We become more sensitive to
> His voice as we divest ourselves of
> worldly distractions. We are better able
> to focus on God and submit to His will.
> This opens the door for the Holy Spirit
> into our lives.

4. Fasting is healthy.

> a. Fasting cleanses your digestive system

from toxins. Doctors consider fasting a cure for certain allergies and diseases. By learning to deny ourselves and exercising discipline, fasting breaks unhealthy addictions in our lives.

5. Be in faith!

a. Prayerfully and thoughtfully ask the Holy Spirit for guidance. Be clear and specific about your faith goals in your personal life, family, finances, and church. These are what you will believe God for during the fast and the entire year to come. Expect God to answer. Maintain a thankful heart throughout and after the fast.

6. Commit to a type of fast.

a. We encourage everyone to commit to a "water only" or a "liquid fast" during this season of prayer and fasting. However, we understand that some are unable to do so because of certain circumstances, such as pregnancy, physically demanding professions, or medical conditions. If you belong to this category, there are alternatives—you may choose to do a combination fast. You may do a liquid fast for three days and then one meal a day fast for the next four, for example, or any other combination according to your need or situation. Pray about the kind of fast you will undertake, consult your physician and commit to it. Do not decide on a day-to-day basis. Commit before the fast, be determined, and ask God for grace.

7. Plan your calendar.

a. Limit your physical and social activities during this period. You need to conserve physical energy and devote more time to prayer and reading the Bible.

8. Prepare spiritually.

a. More than anything, this fast is a time when we believe God for a fresh encounter with Him. Be prepared to have the Holy Spirit put His finger on an area in your life that needs to change. Repentance is the foundation of prayer and fasting. Be ready to repent and change, and be transformed. Surrender everything to Him, and be completely open.

9.   Prepare physically.

a.   Be smart as you enter into this fast. Avoid food that is high in sugar and fat. Prior to the fast, try and eat raw fruit and vegetables only. Consult a physician if you need to.

"Go, gather together all the Jews who are in Susa, and fast for me. Do not eat or drink for three days, night or day. I and my maids will fast as you do. When this is done, I will go to the king, even though it is against the law. And if I perish, I perish" (Esther 4:16).

Fasting reduces the power of self so that the Holy Spirit can do a more intense work within us.

PREPARING to Fast:

1.   Seek the Lord.

   b.   Commit to prayer and Bible reading during the times you usually allocate for meals. The tithe belongs to the Lord. Endeavor to give a tenth of your day [24 hours] which is 2 hours and 40 minutes during your consecration and you will reap the benefits abundantly.

   c.   Join at least one prayer meeting in your local church, prayer group or prayer partners. Corporate prayer is powerful, one can put a thousand to flight and two ten thousand.

   d.   Try and connect with daily prayer meetings scheduled in every local area whether by phone, etc. throughout the fast.

2.   Commit to change.

   b.   Whatever God tells you or puts His finger upon, apply it immediately. If you need to make restitution, immediately contact people to mend broken relationships. If there are habits that need to change, make the adjustment immediately. Ask your group leader to hold you accountable.

3. Practical tips

a. Avoid medical and even natural herbal drugs. However, if you are under medication, these should only be withdrawn upon the advice of your doctor.

b. Limit your physical activity and exercise. If you have a workout routine, adjust it accordingly. A daily two to five-kilometer walk should be your maximum amount of exercise during an extended fast. Please consult your physician.

c. Rest as much as you can.

d. Maintain an attitude of prayer throughout the day. Intercede for your family, pastors, church, nation, our missionaries, world missions, etc.

e. Drink plenty of clean water.

f. As your body adjusts, be prepared for temporary bouts of physical weakness as well as mental annoyances like impatience, irritability, and anxiety. [Withdraw from the withdrawal symptoms.]

g. Reintroduce solid food gradually.

"When you fast, do not look somber as the hypocrites do, for they disfigure their faces to show men they are fasting. I tell you the truth; they have received their reward in full. But when you fast, put oil on your head and wash your face, so that it will not be obvious to men

that you are fasting, but only to your Father, who is unseen; and your
Father, who sees what is done in secret, will reward you"
(Matthew 6:16-18).

"The record of the Bible indicates that prayer and fasting combined constitute the strongest weapon committed to God's believers." Dr. Mary Ruth Swop.

4. Continue praying.

    a. Don't let your prayer life end on the day you finish the fast. Build from the momentum you gained during the fast. Let it transform your prayer and devotional life. Carry the newfound passion with you into every new season.

5. Be expectant.

    a. Be in faith and believe God to answer your prayers soon! Don't give up; persevere in prayer even if you don't see the answers immediately. Make sure you keep the copy of your prayer points. You can check it at the end of the year and see how God has answered your prayers. It can be your thanksgiving list at the end of the year.

"Paul and Barnabas appointed elders for them in each church and, with prayer and fasting, committed them to the Lord, in whom they had put their trust" (Acts 14:23).

> b. Our prayer and fasting give us the opportunity to realign our lives according to His will and consecrate the coming year to Him. As we humble ourselves corporately to Him in prayer, we can expect Him to move mightily in our midst. God's will is for all of us to experience breakthrough and victory in our lives.

> c. Be in faith for God to move miraculously in your life this year beyond what you can ask or imagine. You have a fresh mandate. Be ready to accomplish greater things for God next year and the years to come!

"Now to him who is able to do immeasurably more than all we ask or imagine, according to his power that is at work within us." Ephesians 3:20

6. Spend some time searching the Scriptures and praying.

"Draw nigh to God, and he will draw nigh to you. Cleanse your hands, ye sinners; and purify your hearts, ye double minded. Be afflicted, and mourn, and weep: let your laughter be turned to mourning, and your joy to heaviness. Humble yourselves in the sight of the Lord, and he shall lift you up" (James 4:8-10).

Reflect

Based on John 1:17, where does truth come from?

_____

What did Jesus say we must do so that we can know the truth (John 8:31, 32)?

_____

What is the result of knowing the truth?

_____

Ask God to reveal some lies of the enemy you may have believed that need to be replaced with the truth. Respond and reflect.

_____

_____

_____

_____

_____

_____

_____

_____

_____

ARE YOU READY to begin your seven-day pursuit?

We give ourselves to prayer and fasting as a corporate body, but more so as Watchmen on the wall! For seven days, out of the month of your choice, dedicate to God, soul, mind, body and spirit. YOU WILL DEAL WITH YOUR SPIRITUAL HUNGER FIRST! Jesus promises in Matthew 5:6: *"Blessed are they which do hunger and thirst after righteousness; for they shall be filled."*

The combination of fasting and praying is not a fad or a novelty approach to spiritual discipline. Fasting and praying are not part of a human-engineered method or plan. Fasting and Praying are not the means to manipulate a situation or to create a circumstance. Fasting and praying is a Bible-based discipline that is appropriate for all believers. Fasting and praying break the yoke of bondage and brings about a release of God's presence, power, and provision.

Biblical fasting is going without food, [Abstinence]. The noun translated "fast" or "fasting" is *tsom* in the Hebrew and *nestis* in the Greek language. It means the **voluntary abstinence from food**. The literal Hebrew translation would be **"not to eat."** The literal Greek means to abstain or "no food."

You may decide to go without entertainment and social media outlets. You may put down your television remote or newspaper or perhaps some hobby or form of recreation. I encourage you to add this form of discipline to your fasting, as long as you specifically replace it with prayer. However, to be biblically accurate, fasting has to do with our abstaining from food.

DON'T JUST GIVE IT UP! REPLACE IT! Just to "give up" something is a frivolous approach to fasting. We must replace what we fast from with prayer! Spiritual fasting involves our hearts and the way in which we relate to and trust God.

Fasting gives us discernment and strength to follow through on what God will reveal to us about circumstances in our lives, a direction we are to take, or a command we are to follow.

Control of eating is a valid reason to fast—just not the main reason. The purpose is not the number of pounds you might lose during a fast, but rather, trusting God to help you regain mastery over food during a fast. Jesus said, *"…The spirit indeed is willing, but the flesh is weak" (Matt. 26:41)*.

Fasting is a means of bringing the flesh into submission to the Lord, so He can strengthen us in our mastery over our own selves. Fasting in the flesh makes us stronger to stand against the temptations of the flesh. God's promise is to help us as we overcome the flesh and put all carnal temptations into subjection.

USE THIS DEVOTION GUIDE AS A FOCUS FOR YOUR PRAYER POINTS. This will allow you to CENTER IN PRAYER and receive the promise of agreement.

In conjunction with the daily prayer points, read the Gospel of Saint Mark, two chapters a day for 5 days, then three chapters for the remaining 2 days as a daily devotion and discipline. Prayerfully meditate on the word and the Spirit of God will minister deeply the heart of the Father and Son.

"Again, I say unto you, that if two of you shall agree on earth as touching anything that they shall ask, it shall be done for them of my Father, which is in heaven" (Matthew 18:19).

May His Grace abound to you as His **Sufficiency** becomes your **Efficiency,** in Jesus' name.

ALWAYS REMEMBER TO

- Pray for our leaders, political and ecclesiastical.
- Pray for our nation and families.
- Pray for the economy and that violence and Bloodshed will no longer be heard in our streets.
- Pray for the peace of Jerusalem.

19

Peace, shalom!

> *May the lord bless thee and keep thee; may he cause his face to shine upon thee. May he be gracious unto thee and your house, and grant thee peace; shalom! Numbers 6:24-26*

Privileged to serve and committed to pray.

Sarah Morgan

The Number Seven

The **NUMBER SEVEN** in the Bible represents divine perfection, totality or completion and is mentioned at least 490 times in the Bible.

These are just a few of times it's mentioned in scripture.

- *"On the **Seventh day**, God ended His work which He had made; and He rested on the Seventh day from all His work which He had made. And **God blessed the Seventh Day, and Sanctified it:** because that in it He had rested from all His work which God created and made"* (Genesis 2:2-3).

- **SEVEN YEARS times seven times** is the period between the jubilees (Leviticus 25:8).

- The sprinkling of blood **seven times** (Leviticus 4:6; 14:7).

- The sprinkling of oil **seven times** (Leviticus 14:16).

- The Israelites surrounded Jericho **seven times, and on the seventh day** sounding seven trumpets (Joshua 6:4).

- Elisha's servant looked **seven times** for the appearance of rain (1 Kings 18:43).

- Naaman was required to wash in the Jordan River seven times (1 Kings 5:10).

- The **seven steps** in the temple seen in Ezekiel's vision (Ezekiel 40:22;26).

- Silver was purified **seven times** (Psalms 12:6).

- Worshiping **seven times** a day (Psalms 119:164).

- **Seven maidens** were given to Esther (Esther 2:9).

- **Seven magi** (wise men) (Proverbs 26:16).
- **Seven women** will seek a polyandrous marriage (Isaiah 4:1).
- **Seven lamps and pipes** (Zechariah 4:2).
- **Seven servants** (Greek: diakonoi) in the Jerusalem congregations (Acts 6:3).
- **Seven congregations** in Asia (Revelation 1:4;20).
- **Seven seals** (Revelation 5:1).
- **Seven kings** (Revelation 17:10).
- **Seven stars** (Revelation 1:16, 20; 3:1; Amos 5:8).
- **Seven spirits** (Revelation 1:4; 3:1; 4:5; 5:6).
- **Seven eyes** of the Lord (Zechariah 3:9; 4:10; Revelation 5:6).
- **Seven golden** lampstands (Revelation 1:12).
- **Seven angels** with seven trumpets (Revelation 8:2).

Seven is the number of perfection and completion. As you consecrate these **seven days**, I pray that God will perfect and complete those things concerning you, in Jesus' name.

Day 1

Key Verses: Psalm 138:7-8 (KJV)

Psalm 138:7-8: "*Though I walk in the midst of trouble, thou wilt revive me: thou shalt stretch forth thine hand against the wrath of mine enemies, and thy right hand shall save me. The Lord will* perfect *that which concerneth me: thy mercy, O Lord, endureth for ever: forsake not the works of thine hands.*"

"*8 The Lord will accomplish that which concerns me;*" (AMP)

"*8 The Lord will work out his plans for my life—for your loving- kindness, Lord, continues forever. Don't abandon me—for you made me.*" (NLB)

Psalm 138:7-8 (MSG)
"*7-8 When I walk into the thick of trouble, keep*
*   me alive in the angry turmoil.*
With one hand
*   strike my foes,*
With your other hand
*   save me.*
Finish what you started in me, God. Your love is
*   eternal—don't quit on me now.*"

Prayer Point: Lord, perfect my praise.

Psalms 119:164, "*Seven times a day do I praise thee because of thy righteous judgments.*"
   Psalm 150, "*Praise ye the Lord. Praise God in his sanctuary: praise him in the firmament of his power. Praise him for his mighty acts: praise him according to his excellent greatness. Praise him with the sound of the trumpet: praise him with the psaltery and harp...*"

Psalm 7:17, "*I will* praise *the Lord according to his righteousness: and will sing* praise *to the name of the Lord most high.*"

Psalm 9:1, "*I will* praise *thee, O Lord, with my whole heart; I will shew forth all thy marvelous works.*"

Psalm 9:2, "*I will be glad and rejoice in thee: I will sing* praise *to thy name, O thou most High.*"

Psalm 9:11, "*Sing* praises *to the Lord, which dwelleth in Zion: declare among the people his doings.*"

Psalm 9:14, "*That I may shew forth all thy* praise *in the gates of the daughter of Zion: I will rejoice in thy salvation.*"

Psalm 18:3, "*I will call upon the Lord, who is worthy to be* praised*: so shall I be saved from mine enemies.*"

Psalm 18:49, "*Therefore will I give thanks unto thee, O Lord, among the heathen, and sing* praises *unto thy name.*"

Psalm 21:13, "*Be thou exalted, Lord, in thine own strength: so will we sing and* praise *thy power.*"

Psalm 22:3, "*But thou art holy, O thou that inhabitest the* praises *of Israel.*"

Psalm 22:22, "*I will declare thy name unto my brethren: in the midst of the congregation will I* praise *thee.*"

Psalm 22:23, *"Ye that fear the Lord,* praise *him; all ye the seed of Jacob, glorify him; and fear him, all ye the seed of Israel."*

Psalm 22:25, *"My* praise *shall be of thee in the great congregation: I will pay my vows before them that fear him."*

Psalm 22:26, *"The meek shall eat and be satisfied: they shall* praise *the Lord that seek him: your heart shall live for ever."*

Psalm 27:6, *"And now shall mine head be lifted up above mine enemies round about me: therefore will I offer in his tabernacle sacrifices of joy; I will sing, yea, I will sing* praises *unto the Lord."*

Psalm 28:7, *"The Lord is my strength and my shield; my heart trusted in him, and I am helped: therefore my heart greatly rejoiceth; and with my song will I* praise *him."*

Father God, today I praise You in my sanctuary which is Your Temple, I praise You for Your mighty works in my life. You are great and greatly to be praised, everything within me gives You praise in Jesus' name.

Day 2

Key Verse: 1 Kings 5:10

2 Kings 5:10: *"And Elisha sent a messenger unto him, saying, Go and wash in Jordan seven times, and thy flesh shall come again to thee, and thou shalt be clean."*

Naaman the leper was required to wash in the Jordan River **seven times** and was cleansed and purified from leprosy.

Prayer Point: Lord, perfect my purification.

Numbers 31:19, *"And do ye abide without the camp seven days: whosoever hath killed any person, and whosoever hath touched any slain, purify both yourselves and your captives on the third day, and on the seventh day."*

1 Chronicles 23:28, *"because their/your office was to wait on the sons of Aaron for the service of the house of the Lord, in the courts, and in the chambers, and in the purifying of all holy things, and the work of the service of the house of God;"*

Ezekiel 43:26, *"Seven days shall they purge the altar and purify it; and they shall consecrate themselves."*

Malachi 3:3, *"And He shall sit as a refiner and purifier of silver: and he shall purify the sons of Levi, and purge them as gold and silver, that they may offer unto the Lord an offering in righteousness."*

Titus 2:14, *"Who gave himself for us, that he might redeem us from all iniquity, and purify unto himself a peculiar people, zealous of good works."*

James 4:8, *"Draw nigh to God, and he will draw nigh to you. Cleanse your hands, ye sinners; and purify your heart ye double minded."*

Father God, wash me by the washing of the Word, and **purify** me with perfect purification, in Jesus' name.

Day 3

Key Verse: 1 Kings 18:43

1 Kings 18:43, "and *said to his servant, Go up now, look toward the sea. And he went up, and looked, and said, There is nothing. And he said,* **Go again seven times.**"

Elisha's servant looked **seven times** for the appearance of rain.

Prayer Point: Lord, perfect my patience as I wait for the rain of my blessing.

Psalm 37:7, *"Rest in the Lord, and wait* **patiently** *for him: fret not thyself because of him who prospereth in his way, because of the man who bringeth wicked devices to pass."*

Psalm 40:1, *"I waited* **patiently** *for the Lord; and he inclined unto me, and heard my cry."*

Ecclesiastes 7:8, *"Better is the end of a thing than the beginning thereof and the* **patient** *in spirit is better than the proud in spirit."*

Acts 26:3, *"Especially because I know thee to be expert in all customs and questions which are among the Jews: wherefore I beseech thee to hear me* **patiently**."

Romans 2:7, *"to them who by patient continuance in well doing seek for glory and honor and immortality, eternal life:"*

Romans 12:12, *"Rejoicing in hope; patient in tribulation; continuing instant in prayer;"*

1 Thessalonians 5:14, *"Now we exhort you, brethren, warn them that are unruly, comfort the feebleminded, support the weak, be patient toward all men."*

2 Thessalonians 3:5, *"And the Lord direct your hearts into the love of God, and into the patient waiting for Christ."*

1 Timothy 3:3, *"Not given to wine, no striker, not greedy of filthy lucre; but patient, not a brawler, not covetous;"*

2 Timothy 2:24, *"And the servant of the Lord must not strive; but be gentle unto all men, apt to teach, patient."*

Father God, teach me to wait patiently for every prophetic promise to be birthed in my life in Jesus Name.

Day 4

Key Verse: Joshua 6:4

Joshua 6:4, *"And seven priests shall bear before the ark seven trumpets of rams' horns: and the seventh day ye shall compass the city seven times, and the priests shall blow with the trumpets."*

The Israelites surrounded Jericho **seven times, and on the seventh day** sounding seven trumpets…and the walls came down.

Prayer Point: Lord, perfect my walk of faith till I see my victory.

Romans 4:16, *"Therefore it is of **faith** that it might be by grace; to the end the promise might be sure to all the seed; not to that only which is of the law, but to that also which is of the **faith** of Abraham; who is the father of us all,"*

Romans 4:19, *"And being not weak in **faith**, he considered not his own body now dead, when he was about an hundred years old, neither yet the deadness of Sara's womb:"*

Romans 4:20, *"He Abraham staggered not at the promise of God through unbelief; but was strong in faith, giving glory to God;"*

Romans 5:1, *"Therefore being justified by faith, we have peace with God through our Lord Jesus Christ:"*

Romans 5:2, *"By whom also we have access by faith into this grace wherein we stand, and rejoice in hope of the glory of God."*

Hebrews 10:23, *"Let us hold fast the profession of our faith without wavering; (for he is faithful that promised;)"*

Hebrews 10:38, *"Now the just shall live by faith: but if any man draw back, my soul shall have no pleasure in him."*

Hebrews 11:1, *"Now faith is the substance of things hoped for, the evidence of things not seen."*

Father God, empower me to walk by faith around all my walls of opposition and resistance until I see my perfected victory in Jesus' name.

Day 5

Key Verse: Revelation 1:4

Revelation 1:4, *"John to the seven churches which are in Asia: Grace be unto you, and peace, from him which is, and which was, and which is to come; and from the seven Spirits which are before his throne;"*

Prayer Point: Perfect Your **seven Spirits** in my life.

Revelation 3:1, *"And unto the angel of the church in Sardis write; These things saith he that hath the seven Spirits of God, and the seven stars; I know thy works, that thou hast a name that thou livest, and art dead."*

Revelation 4:5, *"And out of the throne proceeded lightnings and thunderings and voices: and there were seven lamps of fire burning before the throne, which are the seven Spirits of God."*

Isaiah 11:1-3 *"And there shall come forth a rod out of the stem of Jesse, and a Branch shall grow out of his roots:² and the spirit of the Lord shall rest upon him, the spirit of wisdom and understanding, the spirit of counsel and might, the spirit of knowledge and of the fear of the Lord; ³ and shall make him of quick understanding in the fear of the Lord:"*

Father God, let the **seven Spirits** of the Lord rest upon me; the spirit of wisdom and understanding, the spirit of counsel and might, the spirit of knowledge and of the fear of the Lord, in Jesus' name.

Day 6

Key Verse: Genesis 17:1

Genesis 17:1, *"And when Abram was ninety years old and nine, the Lord appeared to Abram, and said unto him, I am the Almighty God; walk before me, and be thou perfect."*

Prayer Point: Perfect my walk with You.

Ephesians 5: 1-2, *"Be ye therefore followers of God, as dear children; and walk in love, as Christ also hath loved us, and hath given himself for us an offering and a sacrifice to God for a sweetsmelling savor."*

Genesis 3:8, *"And they heard the voice of the Lord God walking in the garden in the cool of the day: and Adam and his wife hid themselves from the presence of the Lord God amongst the trees of the garden."*

Genesis 5:22, *"And Enoch walked with God after he begat Methuselah three hundred years, and begat sons and daughters."*

Genesis 5:24, *"And Enoch walked with God: and he was not; for God took him."*

Genesis 6:9, *"These are the generations of Noah: Noah was a just man and perfect in his generations, and Noah **walked** with God."*

Genesis 17:1, *"And when Abram was ninety years old and nine, the Lord appeared to Abram, and said unto him, I am the Almighty God; **walk** before me, and be thou perfect."*

Leviticus 20:23, *"And ye shall not **walk** in the manners of the nation, which I cast out before you: for they committed all these things, and therefore I abhorred them."*

Leviticus 26:3, *"If ye **walk** in my statutes, and keep my commandments, and do them;"*

Leviticus 26:12, *"And I will **walk** among you, and will be your God, and ye shall be my people."*

Father God, empower me to walk uprightly and perfectly before You, in Jesus' name.

Day 7

Key Verse: Genesis 2:2-3.

Genesis 2:2-3, *"On the Seventh day God ended His work which He had made; and He rested on the Seventh day from all His work which He had made. And God blessed the Seventh Day, and Sanctified it: because that in it He had rested from all His work which God created and made."*

Prayer Point: Perfect my rest, perfect my day, perfect my work and perfect everything concerning me and my household on this perfect seventh day.

Matthew 6:33, *"But seek ye first the kingdom of God, and his righteousness; and all these things shall be added unto you."*

Prayer Point: Teach me to seek you first in all things.

Definition:
Seek

- To try and locate or discover: search for.
- To endeavor to obtain or to reach:
- To go to or toward.
- To inquire for: to request,
- To make a search or investigation:

Seek and you shall find.

Deuteronomy 4:29, *"But if from thence thou shalt seek the Lord thy God, thou shalt find him, if thou seek him with all thy heart and with all thy soul."*

Father God, as I seek for you with all my heart and soul, which is my mind, my will, my emotions and being, let me find you in Jesus' name.

2 Chronicles 7:14 *"If my people, which are called by my name, shall humble themselves, and pray, and seek my face, and turn from their wicked ways; then will I hear from heaven, and will forgive their sin, and will heal their land".*

Father God, as one of Your people, called by Your name, I humble myself through fasting and prayer, seeking Your face and not Your hand, repenting, having a change of mind and completely turning from the wicked ways of my heart, thoughts, words and deeds; incline Your ear to hear, forgive me of all my sins and heal every area of our land, in Jesus' name.

Ezra 7:10, *"For Ezra had prepared his heart to seek the law of the Lord, and to do it, and to teach in Israel statutes and judgments."*

Father God, as I have prepared my heart to seek Your Law which is Your Word, give the grace to be a doer of Your Word and likewise teach others, in Jesus' name.

Ezra 8:21, *"Then I proclaimed a fast there, at the river of Ahava, that we might afflict ourselves before our God,* to seek of him a right way for us, *and for our little ones, and for all our substance.*

Father God, as I fast and pray show me the right way to live, the right way to talk, the right way to love, the way to represent you to my little ones and the world in Jesus' name.

Psalm 9:10, *"And they that know thy name will put their trust in thee: for thou, Lord,* hast not forsaken them that seek thee. *"*

Psalm 34:10, *"The young lions do lack, and suffer hunger:* but they that seek the Lord shall not want any good thing. *"*

Psalm 40:16, *"Let all those* that seek thee rejoice and be glad in thee: *let such as love thy salvation say continually, The Lord be magnified."*

Psalm 119:45, *"And I will walk at liberty: for I seek thy precepts."*

Proverbs 8:17, *"I love them that love me; and those that seek me early shall find me*